PENGUIN BOOKS

Shells in Color

Kjell B. Sandved, a native of Norway, came to the United States in 1960 on a research project. During the course of his research, he found working at the Smithsonian Institution so enjoyable that he decided to stay and became an American citizen. This book reflects the full year that he spent looking through and photographing the Smithsonian's collection of ten million shells. Mr. Sandved has been acclaimed for his motion pictures about natural-history subjects, which he continues to produce for the Smithsonian.

Dr. R. Tucker Abbott, a graduate of both Harvard College and George Washington University, is Assistant Director and malacologist for the Delaware Museum of Natural History. His many other books about shells include *American Seashells, Seashells of the World*, and *Seashells of North America*.

SHELLS
IN COLOR
Photographs by Kjell B. Sandved
text by R. Tucker Abbott

PENGUIN BOOKS

Acknowledgments

My thanks to Dr. Harald Rehder, Dr. Joseph Rose-water, Barbara Bedette, and others in the Mollusk Department who assisted and encouraged me in my early years at the Smithsonian Institution.

K. B. S.

I am greatly indebted to the late Gunnar Thorson, renowned marine biologist of Denmark, for giving me permission to reproduce his delightful and informative Christmas card drawings. I hope that his many friends will accept this as a small memorial token of his great contributions to malacology. The drawings were ex-ecuted by Poul H. Winther of Copenhagen.

R. T. A.

Penguin Books
625 Madison Avenue
New York, New York 10022

Penguin Books Canada Ltd,
41 Steelcase Road West
Markham, Ontario, Canada

First published by The Viking Press 1973
Published in Penguin Books 1976

Library of Congress Cataloging in Publication Data

Sandved, Kjell Bloch, 1922—. Shells in color.
  (A Penguin Book)
  (A Studio Book)   Bibliography: p.   Includes index
  1. Shells—Pictorial works.   I. Abbott, Robert
Tucker, 1919—   II. Title.   QL404.S36   1976
594'.04'7   75-41426
ISBN: 0 14 00.4237 7

Text printed in the United States of America by Halliday Lithograph Corporation, West Hanover, Massachusetts. Illustrations printed in Japan by Dai Nippon Printing Company, Ltd.
Bound in the United States of America.

Contents

Contents

Introduction

The eternal yet ever-changing sea that gave birth to the first forms of life still nurtures our planet in a thousand ways. Our weather, our mild temperatures, our rains, even much of the newly created oxygen comes from the oceanic 70 per cent of the earth's surface. Of the half million forms of life in the sea, shells are foremost among the animals in their number of species and varied shapes and colors.

Each shell is a monument to the miraculous and mysterious system of creation. From a biologist's viewpoint, a shell is a frozen and permanent history of the physiology of a once-living mollusk. Among poets, shells have inspired such men as Oliver Wendell Holmes, who wrote "The Chambered Nautilus." Princes and emperors, paupers and merchants, have collected and admired shells for generations.

But to photographers, shells are a particular challenge. Shells are beautiful architectural structures with a story of growth and grace begging to be captured by the camera. Yet the exquisitely detailed sculpturing and rich contrast in colors are also there to be recorded. A change of lighting, a new angle of view, or a variation in background can give a shell an entirely different personality or mood.

Kjell Sandved has created a photographic essay of how shells grow, form, and color their outer homes. First, he shows us the shell in a single all-embracing view—a sort of love-at-first-sight picture—and then step by step he takes us closer to view the wondrous microscopic details of the beads, frosted frills, and color dots that all go into the making of a shell. If you have never collected shells, this book might make you a collector. If you already consider yourself a sort of conchologist, you will see something about shells that I am sure you have never seen before.

Shells Are Living Animals

Shells are the outer limy "skeletons" of soft-bodied mollusks. The snail and the clam grow their protective shells, beginning the day they are born, in very slow, continuous fashion, much as humans grow hair and fingernails.

The eggs of the seashell-producing mollusks are either shed freely into the ocean's water or placed by the female in small protective capsules which are fastened to the bottom. In many marine species the egg hatches into a free-swimming young form that floats off to new territory. Most shells take one or two years to reach maturity. A life span may vary from one to thirty years, depending upon the species.

Snails, conchs, whelks, and other univalves feed with the aid of a long, rasplike ribbon of teeth. Most univalves, like the moon snails, cones, and volutes, are carnivorous, feeding upon worms, crabs, and other mollusks. However, many limpets, turban shells, and some conchs feed solely on seaweeds.

Shell Forms: It may well be said that the perfection of the mathematical beauty of shell forms is such that whatever is most beautiful and regular is also found to be the most efficient and, through the time-honored test of evolution, to be the most useful. The growth of shells is an example of the generating curve; that is, there is a constant increase in the size of the shell while never an alteration of the geometric proportions. The spiral form is almost universal among the snail shells, as indeed it is in many other forms of nature, from the coil of an elephant's tusk to the transitory spiral of a coiled lock of hair. Mathematically speaking, there are several forms of curves, but the two most important are the equable spiral, or spiral of Archimedes, and the equiangular or logarithmic spiral.

The spiral of Archimedes is not common in nature. It may be roughly envisioned by coiling a fire hose or rope tightly around itself on the floor. The width of each coil is the same. It is almost like coiling up a long cylinder. The radius of the entire coil, made up of the successive and equal whorls, will increase in *arithmetical* progression. This type of spiral is seen in some forms of opercula, or trapdoors, that close the apertures of *Trochus* shells.

In contrast to the regular or equable coil is the more beautiful coil formed as the whorls continuously increase in breadth at a steady and unchanging ratio. In 1638 Descartes defined and called it the equiangular spiral. In 1691 Jacques (James, Jacob) Bernoulli called it the logarithmic spiral, while others have named it the geometrical spiral. The spiral coiling can take on many shapes, depending upon how rapidly or slowly the new coils increase their breadth. Thus, a mollusk, such as the abalone (Plate 8) or the Pacific Emerald Nerite (Plates 28–30), may have a shell in which the generating curve grows very rapidly. The early whorls are small, but the later ones are very large. In contrast, as seen in the Sundial Shell on Plate 34, the whorls may increase in breadth very slowly, almost to the point of simulating an Archimedes spiral.

There is a singular property of continued similarity in the growth of the logarithmic spiral. As it grows and is added to, it continues to have the same proportions. A young snail is likely to have the same shape as the larger adult, unless there are other abrupt kinds of growth, such as the development of flaring outer lips (Plates 39 and 41, for example). Aristotle recognized this phenomenon, the adding to an object without changing it, except in magnitude. Thus, if we add to a square an L-shaped portion, shaped like a carpenter's square, we simply end up with a larger square. The Greeks called this a "gnomon." Shells are nothing but continuous gnomonic figures.

Just as the whole shell may have a logarithmic growth, so, too, may patterns of coloration. A fine example is seen in the nerite on Plate 28, where there is a progression of increasing size in the patches and lines of coloration.

Spiral snail shells may be geometrically thought of as three-dimensional cones, expanding at a given rate, and coiled about a common axis. It is a tubular spiral. The shape of the coiled shell may be influenced by several other functions. I have mentioned already the

Figure 1. The life of a gastropod can be a joint enterprise among several classes of invertebrates. Here, *Colus curtus*, a Greenland snail, is carrying on its shell a living sea anemone, *Allantactis parasitica*. Under the foot disc of the sea anemone is a commensal nemertean worm, *Nemertopsis actinophila*, which enters the stomach of its host to steal food.

rate at which the coils (or the mouth of the shell) increase in breadth. But equally important is the plane in which this coiling takes place. If the coiling is on a flat plane, such as a coil of rope on the floor, the shell will be planospiral or shaped like the Nautilus on Plate 100 or the snail on Plate 33. If the whorls descend as they coil, an elongate shell is produced, such as the cerith on Plate 32 or the wentletrap on Plate 35.

Other curious variations in coiling may occur, depending upon how closely or how far apart the succeeding coils obtain. A closely coiled example is seen in most snalis, such as found on Plates 31 and 32, but on the adjacent Plate 33 we see an example of detached coiling, in which the succeeding whorls do not touch the former ones. Random coiling is exemplified by the *Siliquaria* snails shown on Plate 36. Beautiful variations may be produced by a unique outline of the aperture of the shell. In the Miraculous Thatcheria on Plate 91, we see an example in which the outline of the lip is sharply triangular, instead of being a smooth rounded curve. The apex of this triangle forms a conspicuous generating spiral with a ramplike shoulder, resembling some "modern" architectural design.

Shell Material: A sculptor cannot create without clay or stone, nor can a mollusk build its shell without a supply of calcium carbonate, the limestone building blocks for these undersea homes. Through its food, and to some extent by direct absorption from the surrounding water, the mollusk builds up an excess of calcium carbonate in its blood. The tissue responsible for most of the shell deposition is the fleshy, cape-like mantle. This lines the inside of the body whorl of the snail shell or the bivalve, and in some cases, such as in the cowries, may extend up over the outer part of the shell. The liquid calcium carbonate is exuded in between the mantle and the already existing shell. Within moments the liquid begins to crystallize. The crystal lattice may differ, depending upon the various proportions of amino acids and carbon dioxide. There are three crystalline forms of lime in mollusks—calcite, aragonite, and vaterite. Aragonite is a heavy form of lime, and if laid down in thin sheets, it produces mother-of-pearl nacre.

These various forms of crystallized calcium may be laid down in various types of layers, the three most common being: *prismatic* layers, in which the crystals are in the shape of columns; *foliate* or *laminate*, in which the crystals are in sheets only one crystal thick; *crossed laminate*, in which the crystals are locked in two directions with the axes of the crystals being inclined in opposite directions. Equally important in shell formation is the cement or mortar between the crystals. This consists of microscopically thin sheets of organic protein material called *conchiolin*.

Coloration in mollusks may come from pigments, physical refrac-

Figure 2. If one looks carefully at these elongate *Turritella communis* snails half buried in the sand, one can notice the curious small, hooked snails adhering to the base of the shell near the aperture. These are dwarf cap shells, *Capulus hungaricus*, sitting in commensal harmony upon the *Turritella* shells. They feed upon the surplus vegetable detritus gathered by the water currents created by the larger *Turritella* snails.

tion of light rays, or, in the case of certain soft parts, luminous organs. Pigments are manufactured and deposited into the liquid shell material by glands situated along the edge of the mantle. In a snail shell, if a small pigment center continuously produces pigment at one locus, a stripe will be formed as the shell increases in size along the edge of the outer lip. If the pigment center intermittently stops and starts, a long series of dashes or dots may be produced. If the center migrates across the edge of the mantle, an oblique stripe will be produced. By these various activities of the pigment centers, often controlled through inherited genetic factors, all kinds of patterns and colors may be manufactured by the mollusk.

The iridescent coloration of the pearl and the abalone (*Haliotis*) shell is caused by the physical scattering of light that produces a rainbow or nacreous effect. Luminosity is produced in some mollusks by special luminescent cells. Some nudibranch shell-less sea snails when irritated emit flashes of light. A land snail of Japan has a small light organ at the front end of the foot, while the little squid, *Spirula*, has a continuously shining "headlight" at the front end. The siphons of some boring clams, such as *Pholas dactylus*, contain luminescent glands that cause the clam to glow with a dull green light.

Figure 3. Some tiny snails act as parasites, as can be seen here. The tiny white parasitic snails, *Odostomia columbiana*, are extending their small proboscides into the fleshy mantle edges of the larger *Trichotropis* snail. The long, muscular proboscis shows a rhythmical pumping action as it sucks the blood juices from its passive host.

Plate 1. Marine snails must protect their eggs from the thousands of predators that swarm the seas. Fish, crabs, shrimp, and other snails take such a toll of young snails that scarcely a hundredth of those born reach the age of one week. To safeguard the delicate gelatinous eggs, the female snail, such as the Emarginate Dogwinkle from the coast of Oregon, forms tiny yellow urn-shaped capsules of inert, chitinous material. Into each of these she places about a hundred minute eggs and then seals the top. The capsules are formed from a large pore in the sole of the mother's foot. Within a few weeks the young are ready to hatch, not as small crawling snails, but rather as microscopic free-swimming veligers. Veliger snails swim and float through the water with the aid of microscopic hairlike cilia. In about ten days they transform into miniature snails, which have a tiny beginning shell. Dogwinkles do not protect their capsules. The snails live in large colonies on the rocky shores from California to British Columbia. The adult shell ranges from a half to one inch in size. The species shown is *Nucella emarginata* (Deshayes).

Plate 2. Afloat in the open sea, this tiny glob of protoplasm, bearing a shiny, new brown shell, represents the larval form of a *Pinna* clam. Within a week it will settle to a sandy bottom, shed its transparent fleshy lobes, and begin to dig into the sand. Already (on its left) the tiny probing foot is searching for a firm substrate. The adult *Pinna* clams are one to two feet in length, fan-shaped, and quite fragile. The pen shell lives almost completely buried in the sand, with the narrow end down, where it is anchored by a clump of silky threads, the *byssus*.

Plate 3. Pulled from his native West Indian waters, this massive male conch, *Strombus gigas* Linné, unhappily sags from his shell. Below is his brown foot and sharp, chitinous operculum with which he vaults himself along the bottom. To the left is his snout and two tentacles. On the right is his black copulatory verge. Above it is a section of the pink mantle that secretes new shell material. Near the end of the conch's tentacle is an eyestalk mounted by an eyeball that resembles an agate. Conchs can discern light changes and moving objects. They feed on soft, delicate red algae. Their eggs are laid in long, gelatinous strings that become covered with fine sand grains and are therefore difficult to see against a sand bottom. The young conchs, known as "rollers," have a thin, delicate outer lip, but when they mature, a large, thick, flaring lip is developed. For other conchs, see Plates 39 and 41.

Plate 4. Carnivorous snails feed on a great variety of sea creatures, but the triton family, Cymatiidae, prefers members of the starfish class. Here is a West Indian Triton's Trumpet beginning to engulf a starfish. In the Indo-Pacific, the Pacific Triton's Trumpet feeds on the blue *Linkia* starfish and very rarely on the coral-eating Crown-of-Thorns Starfish. The starfish, in turn, feeds on mollusks, usually attacking oysters and scallops, but sometimes swallowing fairly large univalve snails.

Plate 5. Not all mollusks have shells. Several hundred kinds of sea slugs, or nudibranchs, sport their colors in the form of fleshy points, or cerata, some of which contain stinging cells. This Hawaiian *Hermissenda* nudibranch is only an inch in length and lives on colonies of hydroid animals. The life span of a nudibranch is rarely more than two years. They lay many hundreds of thousands of eggs, usually in gelatinous coils colored to match the background on which they were laid. Nudibranchs do not manufacture their own stinging cells, but obtain them by feeding on sea anemones. The tiny balloon-shaped cells, called nematocysts, contain an irritating acid. The nudibranch swallows the stinging cells without breaking them. They are then passed through the gut, up into the fleshy cerata on the back of the animal. There the cells rest, just below the surface of the skin, until they are triggered into discharging their acid by some hungry fish or other molluscan predator.

Plate 6. Feeding by some clams is simply a matter of their pumping water into the mantle cavity. The tiny, floating particles of food stick to the mucous film on the gills of the clam. Thousands of tiny hairs beat the trapped food toward a gutter where it is then shoveled into the mouth by two small fleshy flaps. Here are inch-long Wedge Clams, *Donax denticulata* Linné, of the West Indies that live on the wave-dashed slopes of sand beaches. To the left of the center specimen are two fleshy siphons, the upper one for exhaling, the lower one for inhaling water. To the right is the mobile foot that permits the clam to dig back down into the sand whenever a wave has disturbed it.

Plate 7. The lumbering hermit crab, *Dardanus*, has such a soft "bottom" that it must protect itself from enemies by carrying an old mollusk shell on its back. This Puerto Rican crustacean has chosen an antique Pink Conch for its home. Hermit crabs often quarrel among themselves for better shell homes, with the largest and strongest crabs ending up with the more beautiful houses. Some hermit crabs live on land and carry empty seashells far from the water's edge. If shell collectors put recently cleaned snails out to dry on the ground, hermit crabs are likely to trade their old homes for new ones during the night.

Abalones—the Pearly Sea Ears

At first glance, the broad, open shell of the abalone appears to the novice to be half a clam shell. Closer inspection, however, reveals that these pearly, ear-shaped shells are in reality snail shells, not tightly coiled in a turbanlike tower, but broadly and openly swirling like a donkey's ear. The most immediately recognized characteristic of these strange shells is the series of small perforations on the last whorl. These natural holes serve as an exit for waste waters from the animal's mantle cavity.

The foot of the abalone is very thick and broad, and more than fills the huge aperture of the shell. Abalones are capable of sucking on to the rock bottom with the strength of ten men. Only with the sharp stab of an iron bar can an abalone be dislodged from its substrate. The animal is a vegetarian and grazes on seaweeds found at depths of from ten to two hundred feet.

The foot, when pounded and properly prepared and seasoned, is a delicious sea food, somewhat resembling tender scallops. Abalone are fished and marketed extensively in California, southern Australia, and Japan. A small species is eaten in Europe, but in the West Indies and Florida only two species exist in very deep water, and are no larger than thumbnails.

Plate 8. The three-inch Donkey's Ear, *Haliotis asinina* Linné, shown here, is a familiar abalone of the southwest Pacific. Its interior is a cobalt-blue study in iridescence. Six or seven natural holes remain open, the earlier ones being later sealed. The coiled spire at one end reveals that the abalone is indeed a univalve snail, and not a clam valve. (See Plate 11.) The early holes in the spire are completely sealed over. What once were open perforations through which passed water are now oval mounds of shelly material. Like all snail shells, the abalone's shell starts with a smooth, tiny nucleus. Around it grows each succeeding coil with its geometrically expanding cords and threads.

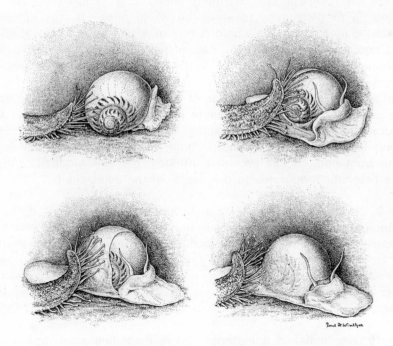

Figure 4. A moon snail has a unique protection against greedy starfish bent on devouring it. As soon as the tubular feet of the starfish approach the snail, the moon snail extends a fleshy cape up over the back of its shell. Thus enveloped in a mucous sheath, the snail is able to glide away to safety.

Through the Keyhole

Keyhole Limpets are charming shells that children delight in holding up to their eyes to view the world anew. It was nature's enchanting idea to bless a whole family of rock-dwelling limpets with this singular characteristic. The natural hole serves a very important physiological function, for it is through this orifice that all waste products and all eggs and sperm are shed into the open ocean. There are more than three hundred kinds of keyhole limpets, ranging in size from one-half inch to five inches in length. They live on rocks, are nocturnal in habit, and feed exclusively on fine seaweeds. Young keyhole limpets are born without a "hole." Early in life a slot develops at the front end, and as growth continues, the slot gradually forms into a hole which migrates to the center of the adult shell.

Plate 9. Closely related to the keyhole limpets are the small, delicate slit limpets that have a small slot in the front end of the shell, serving the same purpose as does the central keyhole. This quarter-inch Philippine *Emarginula* is one of the few mineral collectors among the mollusks. What appear to be specks of dirt on the surface of this slit limpet are actually fine grains of sand welded to the shell by the animal.

Plate 10. Like polished gemstones, these magnified sand grains are carefully lined up on the surface of the delicate slit limpet. The cementing process is begun by the edge of the fleshy mantle which exudes liquefied calcium carbonate. The sand grain is held in place by the mantle, and the "glue" hardens within a few minutes.

Plate 11. A magnified view of the beginning whorls of a Donkey's Ear Abalone (*Haliotis asinina* Linné) from the Philippines. (Also see Plate 8.) The nuclear whorls are smooth and coiled like those on a regular snail's shell. To the right can be seen the oval breathing holes that have been sealed over with shelly material as the animal has grown larger.

Plate 12. The inch-long Red-rayed Keyhole Limpet, *Fissurella scutella* Gmelin, abounds on the rocky shores of South Africa. This species is characterized by more than a dozen rich red-brown rays of color that fan out from the central "keyhole."

Figure 5. A cockle has a most extraordinary ability to leap through the water by first extending its long red foot and then snapping it back in the opposite direction. Evidently this is a natural escape mechanism used to avoid predacious starfish.

The Patella Limpets

Resembling a Roman shield, the strong oval shell of the limpet protects the soft body of the snail hidden beneath it. The streamlined shape, not unlike the patella knee bone of humans, is an adaptation to the rigorous, wave-dashed conditions of the rocky seacoasts. The limpets vary in size, from tiny, delicate species living on brown seaweed and resembling wheat chaff, to the heavy white eight-inch Giant Mexican Limpets that live in the swirling waters of the coast of the Gulf of California. A large, flat muscular foot keeps the limpet attached to the rock surface with tremendous force. Only a quick thrust of a knife will dislodge it. Limpets are nocturnal, usually grazing on microscopic seaweeds when the tide is out and the sun has gone down. Some species wear down an oval indentation in the rock and, after a night of foraging, return to their rocky roosts. The tiny radular teeth, used to scrape up food, have a high amount of magnetite, an iron oxide, to prevent excessive wear.

There are about 150 species belonging to several families, the two most abundant being the Patellidae and the Acmaeidae. Limpets abound in cool waters along rocky coasts. New Zealand, South Africa, western North America, and northwest Europe possess most of the species.

Plate 13. The underside of the Sweet Limpet, *Patelloida saccharina* (Linné), from the Indo-Pacific shows a brown-flecked central scar where the muscles and soft parts are attached to the shell. This is a common rock-dweller of tropical coasts, usually reaching a length of three quarters of an inch.

Plate 14. Some species of limpets develop strong, rounded ribs that add to the strength of the shell, as demonstrated by the inch-long Hawaiian Limpet, *Cellana exarata* Nuttall. This is the light-colored form, *lutrata* Nuttall.

Plate 15. The small delicate Frosty Limpet, *Helcion pruinosus* Krauss, from South Africa lives in the crevices and underhangings of rock ledges. It is moderately common and grows to an inch in size.

Figure 6. The giant *Cymbium* volutes off the coast of West Africa are collected for food by natives. The volute feeds on bivalves. The center figure shows a volute, on its back, clasping a bivalve and beginning to devour it. At the lower left can be seen several miniature volutes that have just been born alive from their mother's oviduct.

Plate 16. This underside view of a dark specimen of the Hawaiian Limpet, *Cellana exarata* Nuttall, displays its patterns of strong radial ribs. This species was possibly introduced accidentally from the Bonin Islands, off Japan, centuries ago. They have been found clinging to the bottoms of ships. In Hawaii, where they were once very abundant, they are eaten raw in a sauce.

Plate 17. The rays of a limpet are tracks of pigment cells located intermittently along the periphery of the mantle. As shell material is added to the edge, pigments are diffused into the calcium carbonate. This common species from Japan, the Black-lined Limpet, *Cellana nigrolineata* Reeve, is three inches long.

Top and Pheasant Shells, and Nerites

The buttonlike top shells are renowned for their intricate beading and bright colors. The interior of these aragonite shells are nacreous, and the larger species, such as the *Trochus* of the southwest Pacific, have been a source of pearly material for buttons and brooches. Top shells have a trapdoor of chitinous material, while their turban relatives of the family Turbinidae have large, heavy, shelly opercula. Pheasant shells of the family Phasianellidae rarely exceed an inch in size. They are vegetarians, and their trapdoor is calcareous.

Plate 18. The small Multicolored Top Shell from the shores of South Africa sports a variety of bright colors. This is *Gibbula multicolor* (Krauss), one of nine species in that area. It seldom exceeds half an inch in diameter.

Plate 19. The common southwest Pacific Strawberry Top Shell, *Clanculus pharaonius* (Linné), is a study in beading. This inch-long snail lives under rocks on intertidal reef flats. (See also Plate 22.)

Plate 20. The uncommon *Clanculus flosculus* (Fischer) is an inch-size beaded jewel from the Indian Ocean. Details of its structure are magnified in Plate 24.

Plate 21. The kelp snails of southern Australia and Tasmania are commonly washed ashore after storms. They are gathered in large numbers by shaking the stranded weed over buckets. The shells are dipped briefly in acid to remove the outer coating, thus exposing the opal-like, iridescent underlayers. The cleaned shells are strung into necklaces. Pictured here is a common half-inch-long *Phasianotrochus leucostigma* (Menke) from South Australia.

Plate 22. A close-up view of *Clanculus pharaonius* (Linné), the Strawberry Top Shell shown in Plate 19.

Plate 23. Pheasant shells are related to the turban shells. They have a shelly operculum that closes the aperture of the shell. There are about three dozen species, most living among weeds in shallow water. The largest come from southern Australia, but South Africa has a few very common species. Clouded spotting is a common characteristic throughout the family Phasianellidae. This common one-third-inch South African species has many scientific names, but *Phasianella capensis* (Dunker) appears to be the earliest valid one. Plate 25 shows the graceful form of the entire shell.

Plate 24. A close-up view of *Clanculus flosculus* (Fischer) shows the extraordinary regularity of the production of spiral rows of colorful beads on the surface of the body whorl of the top shell seen in Plate 20.

Plate 25. Adult shell of *Phasianella capensis* (Dunker) from South Africa. It is only one-third inch in length. (Also see description of Plate 23.)

Plates 26 and 27. The buttonlike *Umbonium* shells are very abundant in southeast Asia. They are low and flat, with a highly glossed surface, and with a buttonlike callus on the underside. This is the half-inch, very common, and very variable *Umbonium vestiarium* (Linné).

Plates 28–30. The regular irregularity of the pigment patterns that characterize the nerite family are shown to great advantage in the tiny Pacific Emerald Nerite. Three or four types of color pigments are laid down at the edge of the growing shell. A green background is continuously produced. Some color cells produce snow white for a short while, then abruptly lay down black or red pigments. *Smaragdia rangiana* (Récluz), a quarter-inch snail, lives on the blades of green sea grasses and is thus difficult to see. All nerites are vegetarians. They have a shelly operculum, or trapdoor, that can completely seal the entrance to the shell. Almost all of the hundred-or-so species are shallow-water dwellers. Many live on intertidal rocks, while several dozen species live in estuarine rivers or small tropical rivers. One species in Melanesia regularly climbs mangrove trees, but must return to the sea to lay its tiny egg capsules.

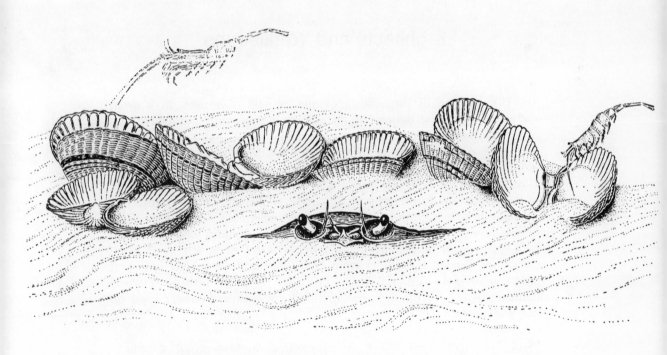

Figure 7. Bivalves fall prey to many enemies. The green crab, *Carcinus maenas*, is one of the most voracious predators of the European cockle, *Cardium lamarcki*. One crab can devour a half-dozen cockles in twenty-four hours. The common shrimp, *Crangon crangon*, acts as a jackal and cleans out the few meat remnants.

Architects and Wentletraps

The swirling of the whorls of snail shells may take on a great variety of form and degree. If the whorls grow about themselves on about the same plane, a very flat, discoidal shell results, as seen in Plates 33 and 34. If the whorls descend or drop down as they wrap around each other, a turreted or pointed shell results, as shown in Plates 31 and 32. Tortuous patterns of irregular coiling are exemplified in the corkscrew formations of *Siliquaria* snails shown on Plate 36.

Wentletraps of the family Epitoniidae resemble spiral stairways, hence their Dutch name "wenteltreppe." Their graceful whorls marked by regular axial blades have been admired by generations of shell collectors. During the 1700s wentletraps brought very high prices at shell auctions in Holland. There are now more than three hundred known species in this fascinating family. Wentletrap snails feed on sea anemones.

Plate 31. Periwinkles are a well-known, ubiquitous group of shore snails. In Europe they have been sold by the basketful in fish markets for many generations. The word "periwinkle" comes from the earlier Elizabethan words "penny winkle," meaning winkles or small whelks that cost only a penny per handful. Periwinkles of the family Littorinidae are common throughout the world wherever there are intertidal, rocky shores. The Papillose Periwinkle, *Tectarius rugosus* (Wood), shown here, is limited to the southwest Pacific area. This inch-long turbinate shell is found above the high-tide mark, usually under the shade of overhanging trees near the shore. The back lighting supplied by the photographer gives this specimen an ethereal quality.

Plate 32. The horn shells are predominantly an estuarine family, preferring the hot brackish waters of the muddy mangrove swamps of the tropics. They are found in colonies of millions of specimens, on the glistening black, muddy flats where oceanic salt waters mix with the nitrogenously rich fresh waters from large rivers. Some species, such as the Finned Horn Shell, *Cerithidea cingulata* (Gmelin), shown here, are capable of carrying intestinal parasites of humans. This inch-long species lives from Japan southward throughout southeast Asia and the East Indies. It is a favorite food of aquatic birds and estuarine fish.

Plate 33. This dainty, deep-sea species is an outstanding example of unattached whorling. Less than a quarter-inch across, this glasslike snail shell lives a solitary life many hundreds of fathoms deep in the Bay of Bengal. It belongs to the genus *Spirolaxis.*

Plate 34. Within the center of this gorgeous Sundial Shell from the Pacific is a tiny, glassy nuclear whorl that represents the beginning of life for this specimen. Once hatched from its egg, this minute glossy whorl, armed with a ciliated foot, swims freely through the oceanic waters for several weeks. After an adventurous journey on the high seas, the minute snail metamorphoses into a heavier shell and sinks to the bottom to begin a normal life. This is a widely distributed Indo-Pacific species, an inch and a half in diameter, called *Architectonica perspectivum* (Linné).

Plate 35. There are probably more than three hundred kinds of wentletraps found throughout the world. This slender beauty, less than two inches in length, is not uncommonly dredged from the inky depths off Japan, from five to ten fathoms. It is the Marked Wentletrap, *Epitonium stigmaticum* (Pilsbry), a moderately common species, so named because of the soft brown markings between the white ribs.

Plate 36. It may take two to tango, but for the strange worm shells, *Siliquaria anguina* (Linné), it is not uncommon for them to become entwined in this fashion. Normally they are associated with soft sponges and live in large colonial masses. Characteristic of this genus is a long, longitudinal, open slit running along the entire length of the shell and through which water may pass. This species is common in deep water throughout the southwest Pacific, from Japan to Australia.

Plate 37. The squat Threaded Wentletrap from Japan, *Epitonium latifasciatum* (Sowerby), is an inch-long beauty marked with three delicate spiral bands of brown, and numerous white reinforcing axial ribs. This shell is commonly dredged off the coast of Japan between five and ten fathoms.

Plate 38. Most famous of all the wentletraps is the three-inch Precious Wentletrap, *Epitonium scalare* (Linné), known to the early shell collectors of Europe as a fabulous collector's item. Huge sums were paid at eighteenth-century auctions for this unique alabaster shell. Legend has it that clever Chinese merchants made counterfeit specimens of rice paste, but to date no authentic "fakes" have been discovered. The species lives in the southwest Pacific and may now be obtained commercially for a few dollars.

Conchs and Moon Snails

Conchs (pronounced "konks") are large marine snails, many of which are edible and a few of which are used as trumpets by primitive peoples. The true conchs belong to the family Strombidae, a group of marine shells living in the tropics, that are characterized by flaring outer lips, long eyestalks, and sickle-shaped opercula. In the West Indies the foot-long Pink Conch (see Plate 3) is a main source of protein food for the Bahama fishermen and villagers. There are about eighty-five kinds of *Strombus* conchs throughout the world. The Indo-Pacific area, stretching from the eastern shores of Africa to Polynesia, has the greatest number. All are vegetarians, and they generally live in large colonies in shallow water where there is an ample supply of seaweeds.

Moon snails are carnivores and are capable of grasping a bivalve in their large, fleshy foot and with their proboscis drilling a hole through the clam's hard shell. Moon snails lay their eggs in a sandy collar of gelatinous material resembling a coiled section of wide ribbon. The family Naticidae contains genera with soft, chitinous opercula, as well as those that are made up of shelly material.

Plate 39. The Variable Conch, *Strombus mutabilis* Swainson, has a distribution extending from Africa to Polynesia. The curious, zebralike color form shown here is limited to the western Pacific Arc, a zoological region extending from southern Japan to Indonesia and eastward to Fiji. Note the weakly U-shaped embayment in the lower part of the outer lip. This is known as the "stromboid notch," a characteristic common to most Strombidae.

Plate 40. Perhaps the most agile of the members of the Strombidae is this slender, glossy *Terebellum terebellum* (Linné) that can zip through the water when alarmed by an enemy. It also has the ability to crawl beneath the surface of the sand, but at the same time keep watch on the world above by protruding one of its eyes up above the surface, much like a periscope. This two-inch spotted shell is widely distributed throughout the tropical Indo-Pacific. Its color patterns are very variable, sometimes having zebralike stripes.

Plate 41. Among the very uncommon *Strombus* conchs of the Pacific is the Vomer Conch of the southwest Pacific. Its optimum habitat seems to be in New Caledonia, although many specimens are found each year in the Ryukyu Islands off China. This three-inch stunning shell has the most delicate spiral lines on the inside of the outer lip. A rare form, *Strombus vomer* Röding, subspecies *hawaiiensis* Pilsbry, is limited to the Hawaiian chain of islands.

Plate 42. The early French naturalist, Lamarck, first named this attractive moon snail of the Philippines. He appropriately dubbed it *Natica zebra*. It is a moderately common species and reaches a length of one inch.

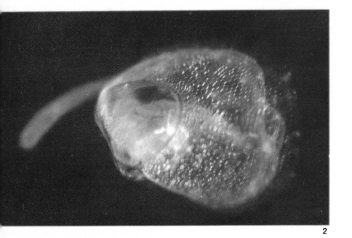

2

3

4

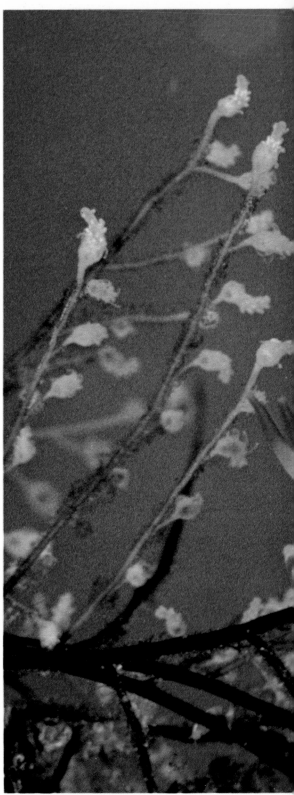

5

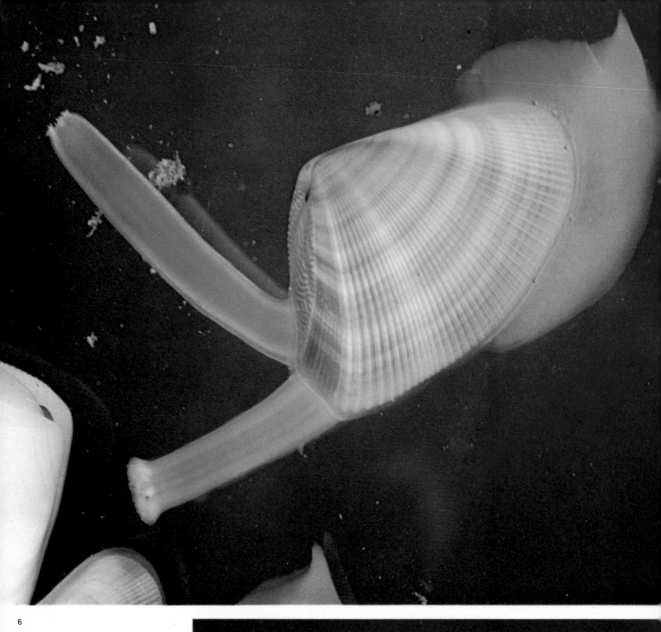

6

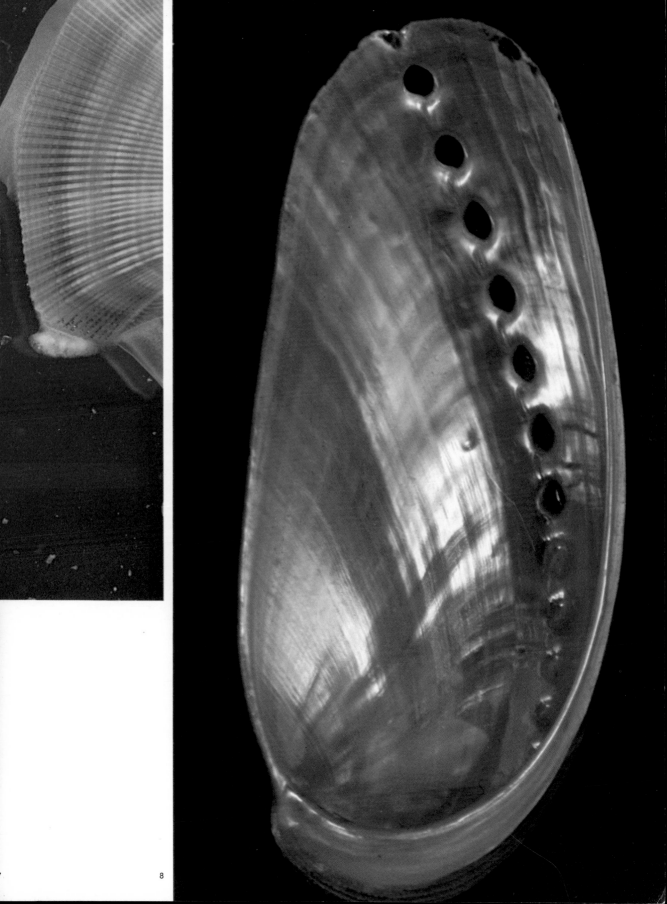

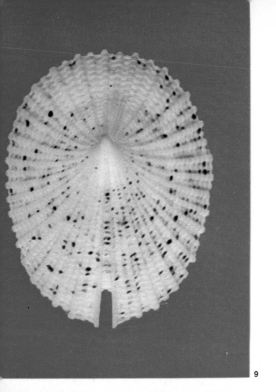

9

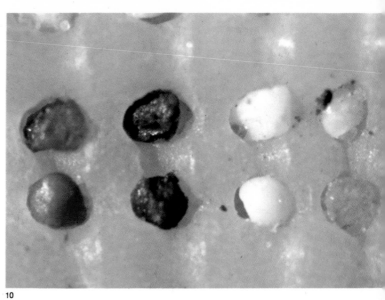

10

11

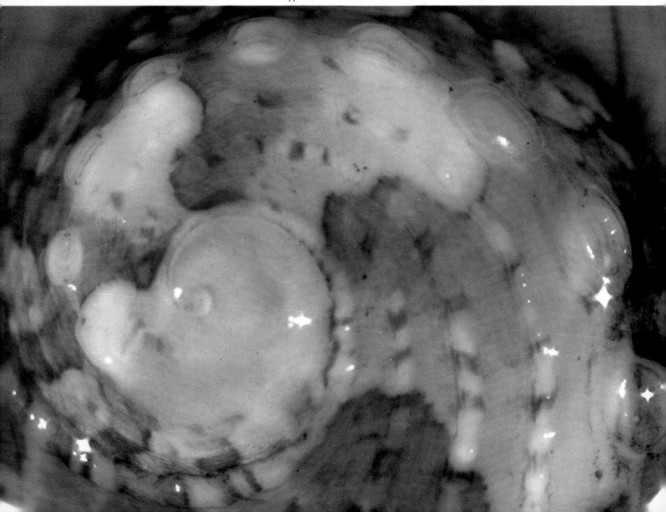

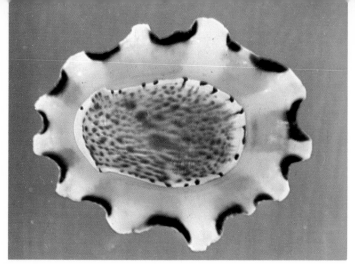

13

14 15

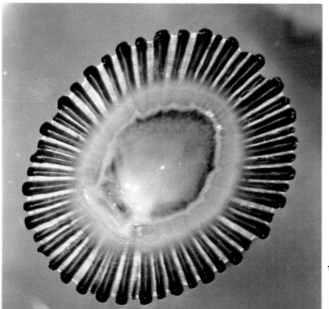

16

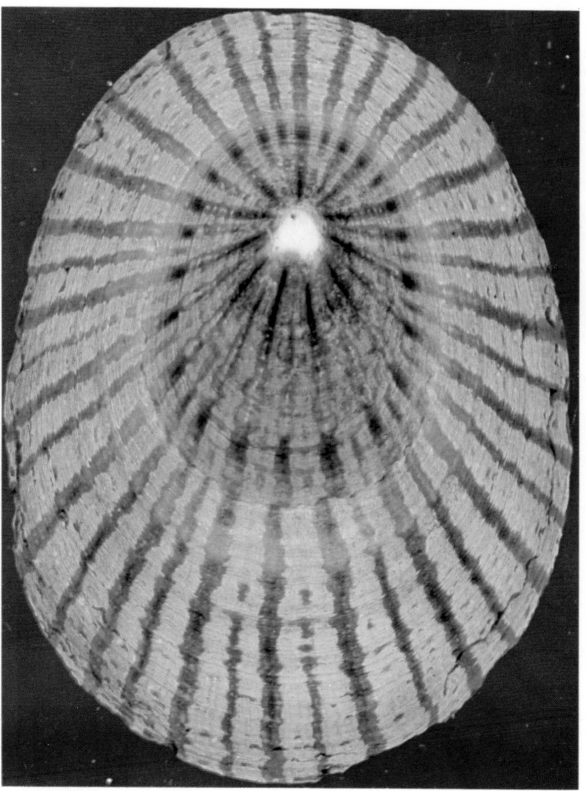

17

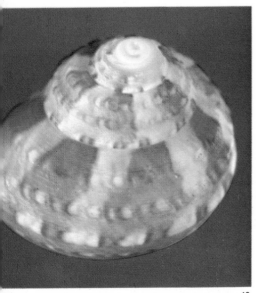

18   19

20

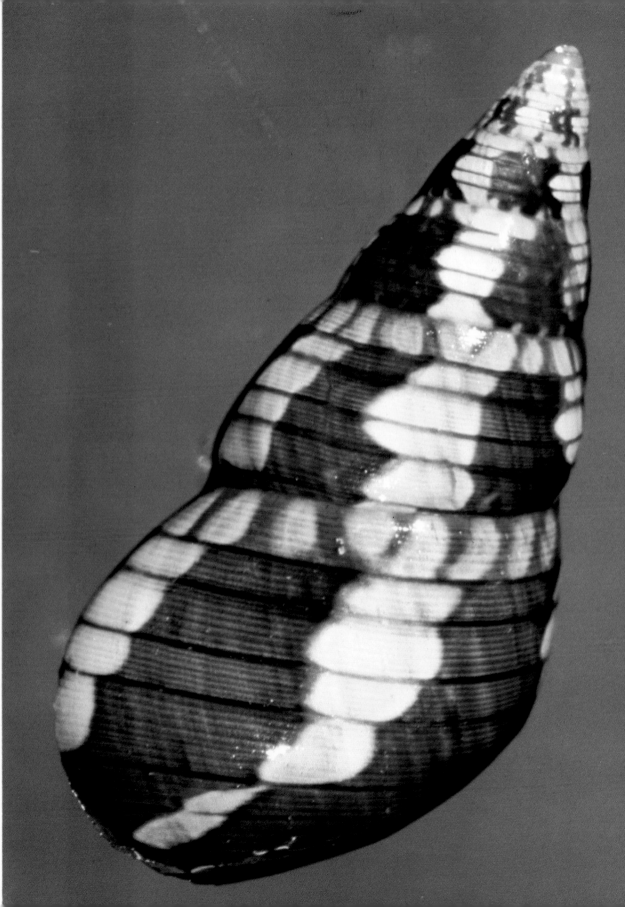

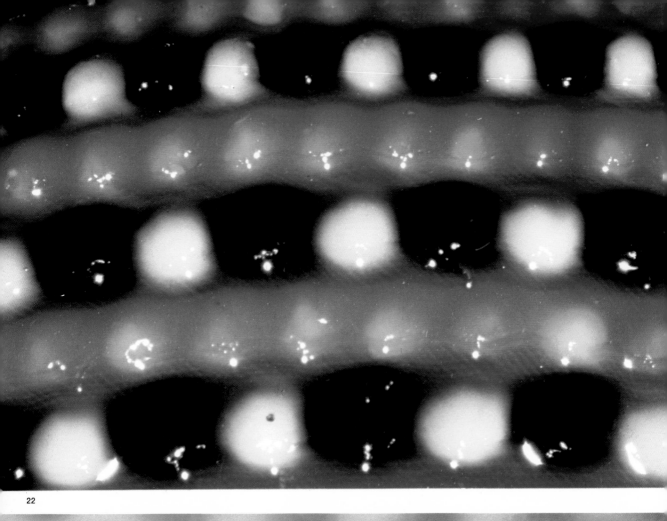

22

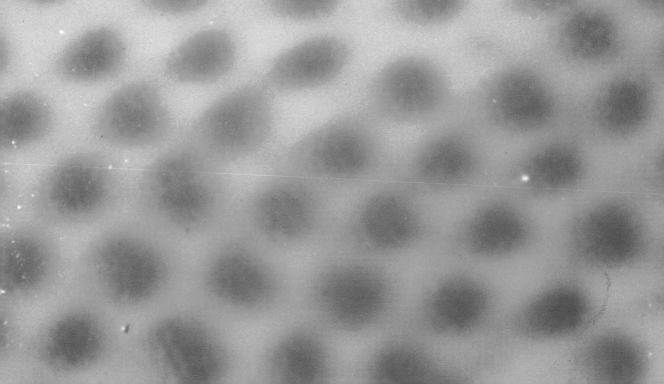

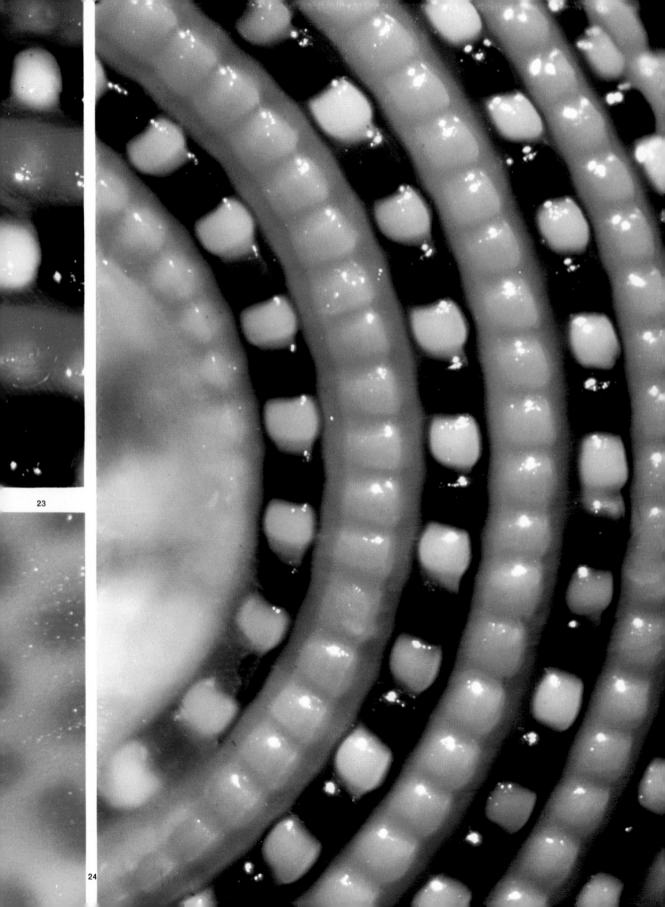

23

24

31

32

33

34

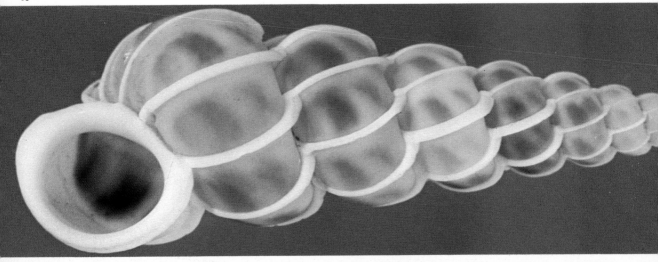

40

41

42

39

43

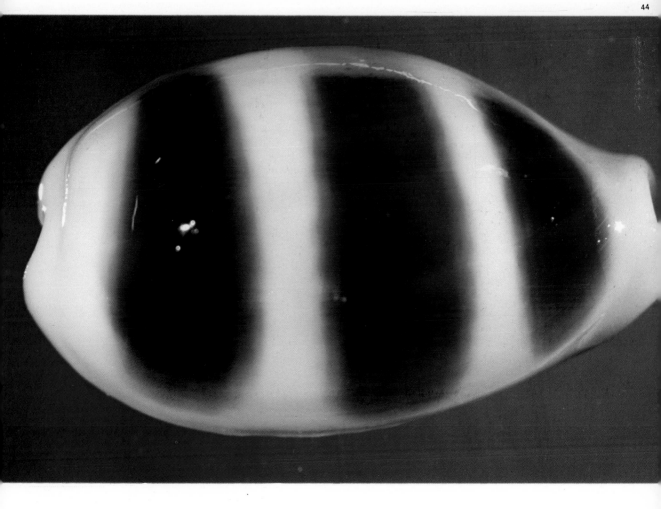

50

51

52

53

54

55

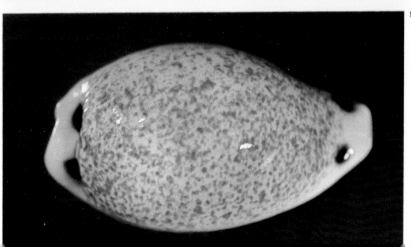

58

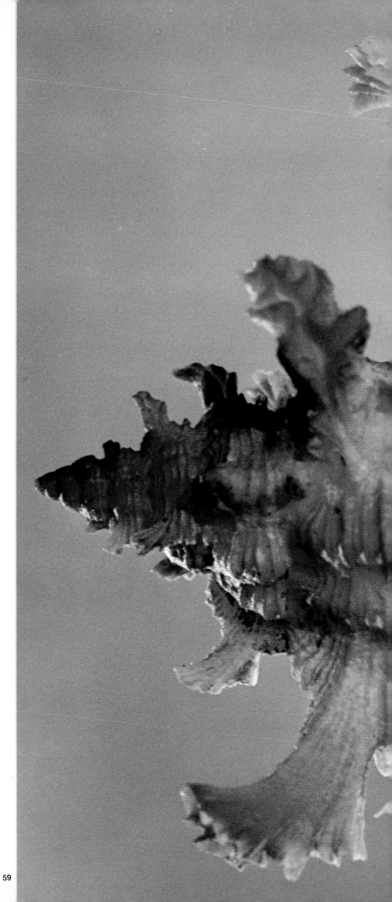

59

60

61

62

63

64

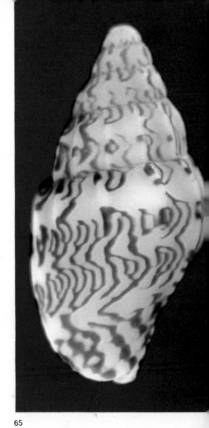

65

66

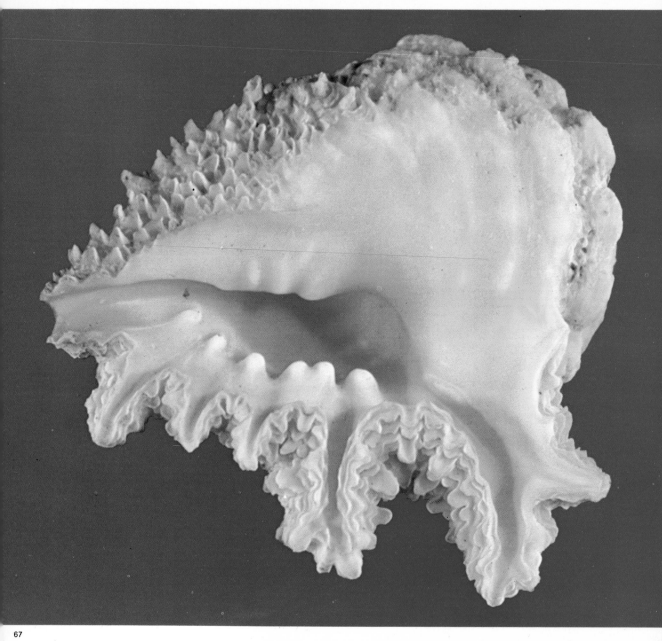

67

68

69

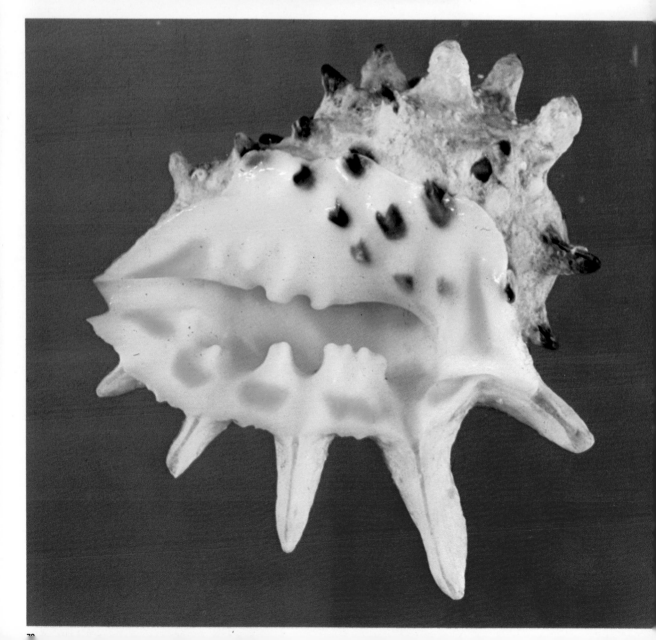

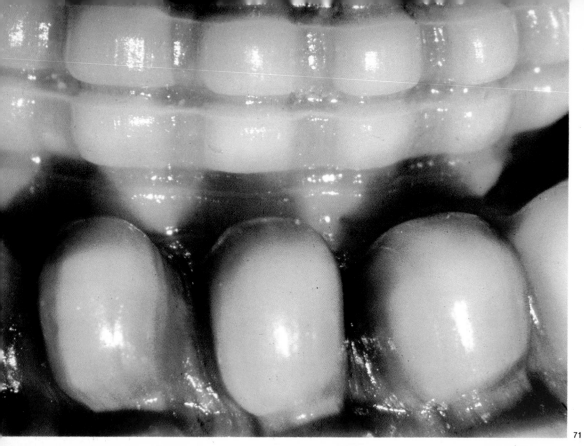

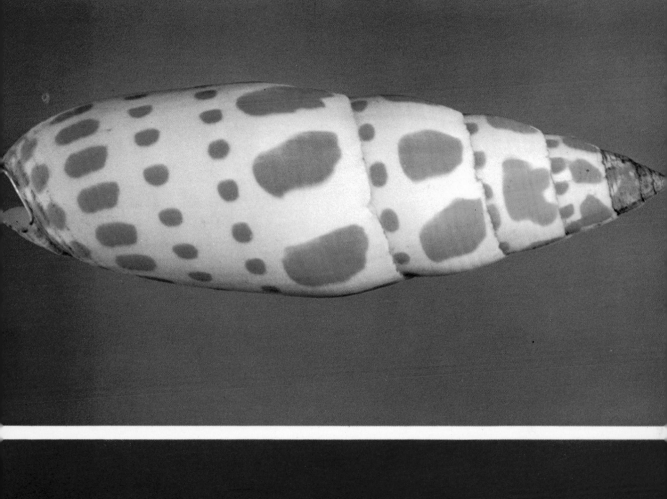

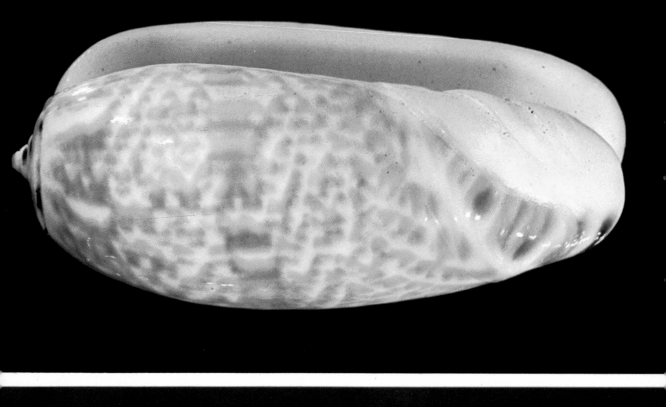

78

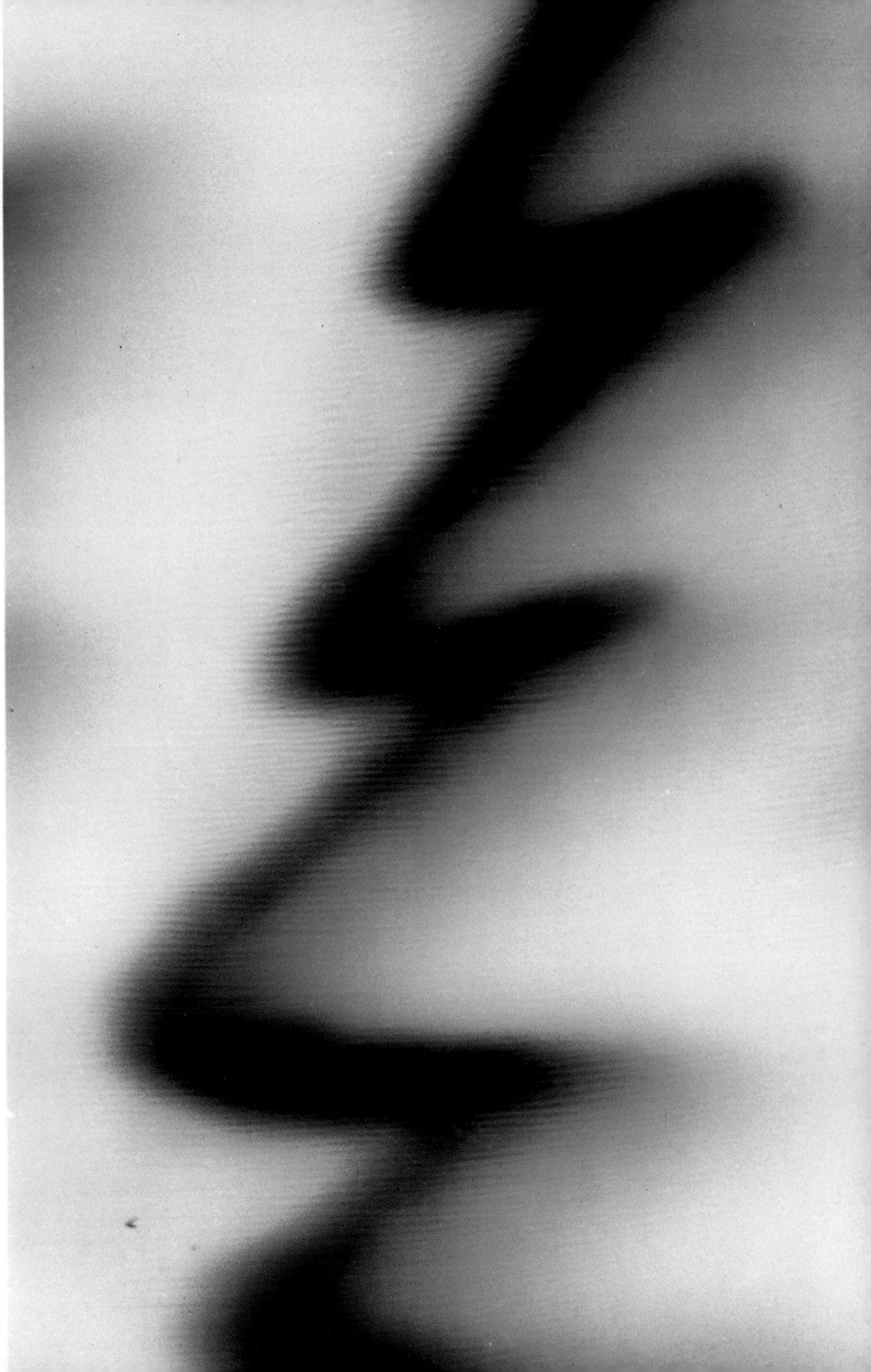

79

80

81

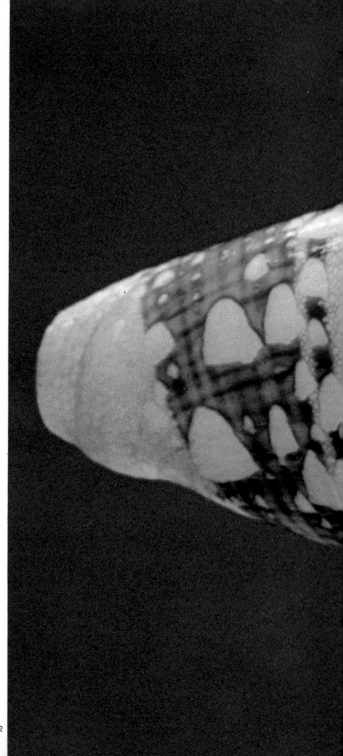

82

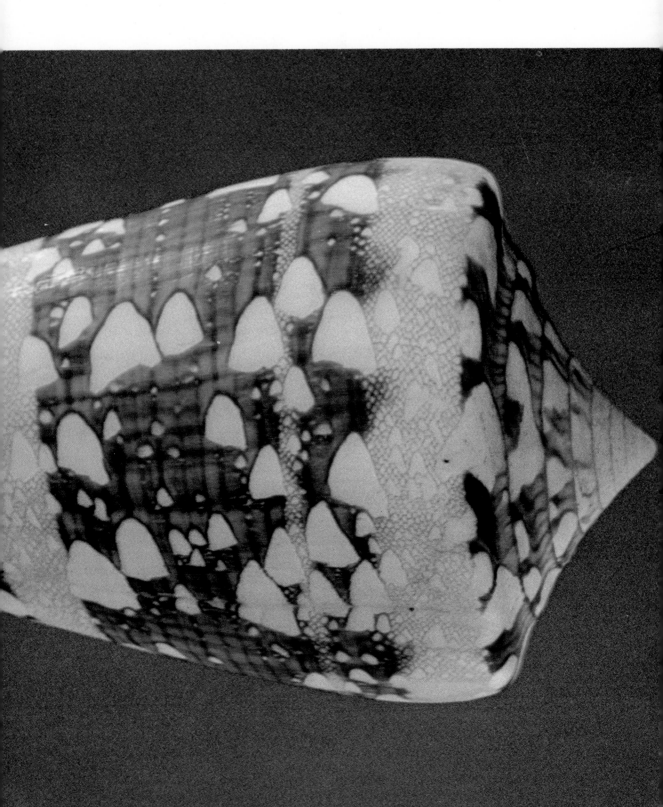

83

84

86

85

87

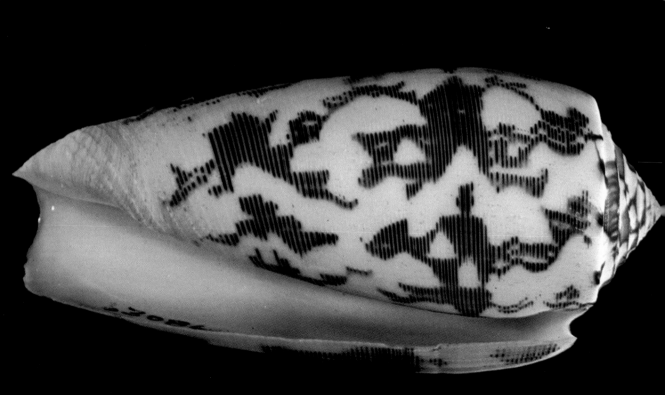

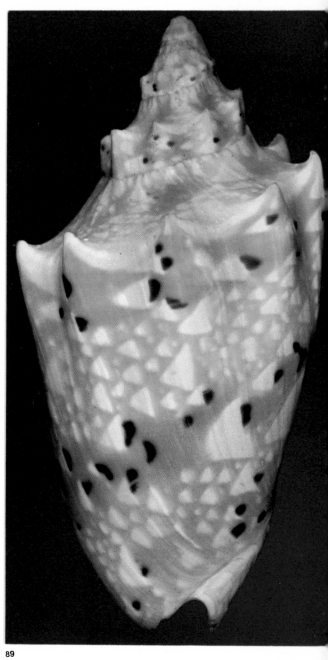

89

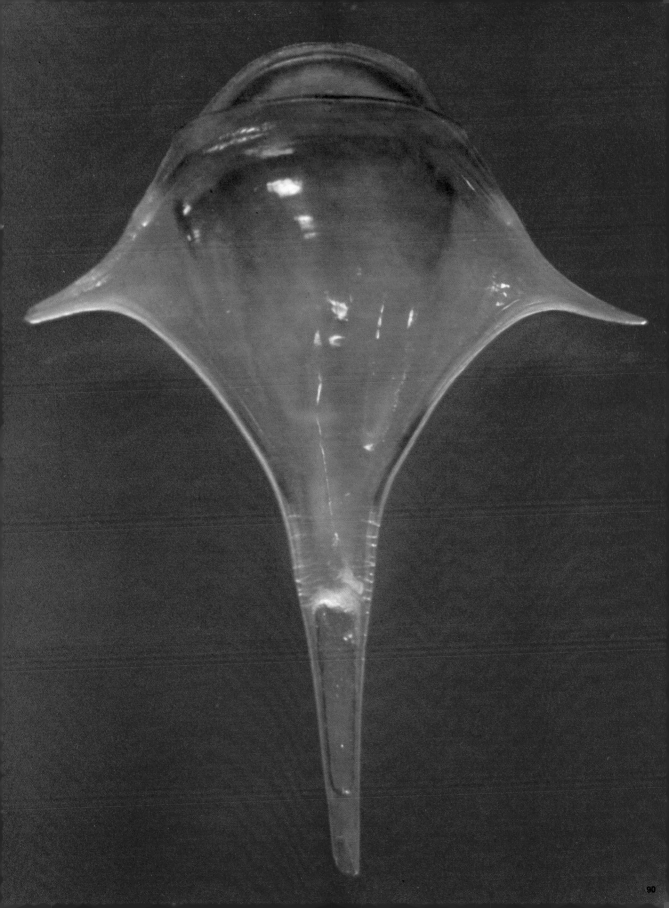

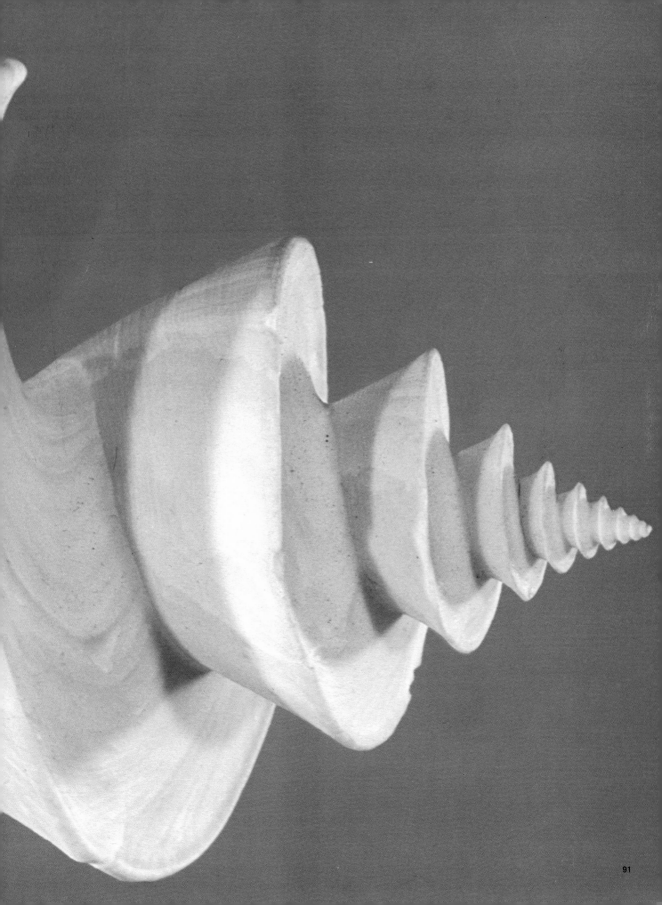

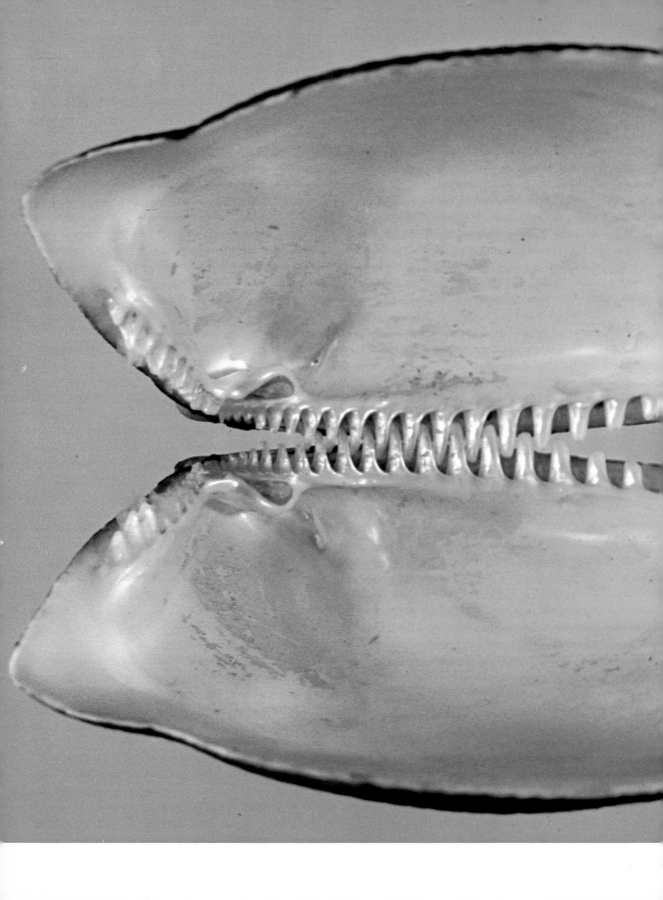

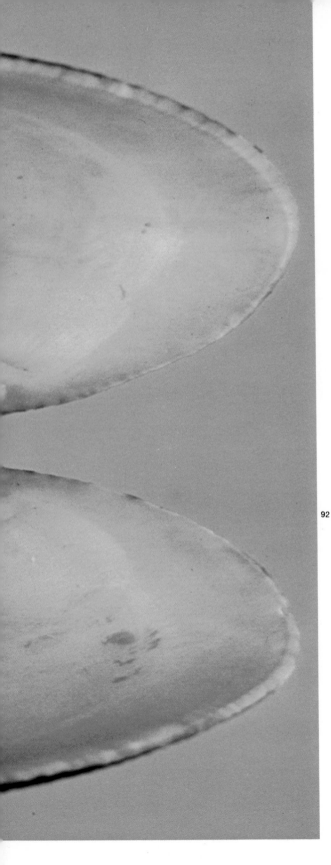

92   93

94

95

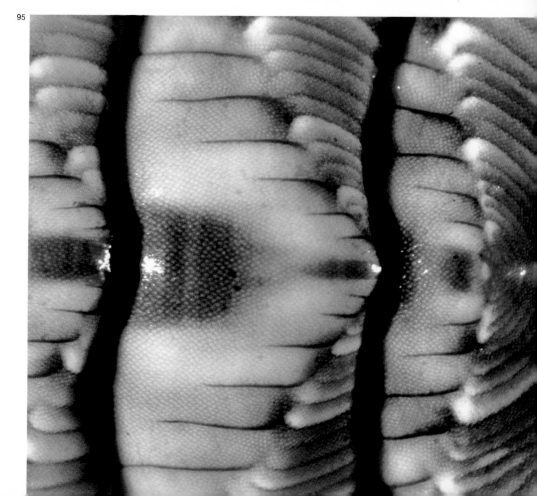

97

98

99

Cowries-Jewels of the Depths

"Jewels of the depths" is the appropriate and customary nickname applied to this resplendent group of glossy shells. Because the fleshy mantle of the animal extends over the outer surface of the shell, the cowries have a beautifully shiny and colorful finish. The natural gloss almost suggests that these shells have been artifically polished. Cowries have been used by primitive man as money, and by early civilizations as symbols of life, rebirth, and sexual virility. There are about 180 living species. No museum or collector has ever acquired all known species and races.

Plate 43. This two-inch lovely species has a very wide range, from East Africa to Clipperton and Tahiti islands. It lives deeply embedded in the fluted coral heads of *Porites lobata*, usually at depths ranging from fifteen to thirty feet. *Cypraea scurra* Gmelin is an uncommon species. Note the sharpness of the dots on the back, but the subdued. hazy blotches on the lower edges of the shell.

Plate 44. This well-known little cowrie, *Cypraea asellus* Linné is readily recognized by the three broad black bands across the upper surface. It is commonly found in shallow water among stones, from eastern Africa to the central Pacific.

Plate 45. Just under an inch in length, this exquisite species, *Cypraea lutea* Gmelin, has an opposite side of charming zigzag lines. This cowrie has a bright-orange mantle. It is moderately common in the southwest Pacific.

Plate 46. The Sieve Cowrie is a masterpiece of circular white dots on a black-brown background. Known throughout the Indo-Pacific since earliest times, it was given the name *Cypraea cribraria* by the Swedish naturalist Linnaeus in 1758.

Plate 47. Children's Cowrie was discovered in 1825, yet less than a thousand specimens have turned up in the past hundred years. It is an inch-long wondrous cowrie, characterized by about two dozen strongly raised plaits of rusty-brown. It is an uncommon Indo-Pacific species, best known from eastern Polynesia.

Plate 48. There is probably no more distinct or more geographically limited cowrie than the famous Ocellate Cowrie, known only from the shores of the subcontinent of India. The tiny black dots located within the larger white circles on the backs of this cowrie are immediate clues to its identity as *Cypraea ocellata* Linné. It is moderately common in shallow water within its confined range.

Plate 49. Gaskoin's Cowrie, *Cypraea gaskoini* Reeve, described in 1846, is found in Hawaii and Fiji. Its most favorable habitat is among broken coral from about fifty to eighty feet in depth. The mantle and foot are a vivid carmine-red. Dr. C. M. Burgess, the Hawaiian expert on cowries, says that the egg capsules are orange-yellow and are laid in clusters of about one hundred.

Plate 50. A magnified detail of *Cypraea irrorata* Gray shown in its entirety on Plate 54.

Plate 51. A close-up view of *Cypraea limacina* Lamarck from the Indo-Pacific shows the curious raised white spots along the side of the shell.

Plates 52 and 53. The well-known and common *Cypraea isabella* Linné was named because of its drab and dirty-gray appearance. Queen Isabel of Spain had instructed her female courtiers not to change their underwear during the battle of Granada until final victory. Victory never came, and custom had it throughout the rest of Europe that garments unwashed and gray could appropriately be called "isabelline." This species reached a length of about two inches and is moderately common throughout the entire Indo-Pacific region.

Plate 54. This half-inch gem has very delicate spottings. *Cypraea irrorata* Gray comes only from eastern Melanesia and Polynesia.

Plate 55. The Four-spotted Cowrie, *Cypraea quadrimaculata* Gray, from the southwest Pacific is only an inch in size and is characterized by two black spots at each end of the shell. It is uncommon.

Frog Shells

Plate 56. The Robin Redbreast Triton, *Cymatium rubeculum* (Linné), of the southwest Pacific, is a two-inch colorful shell of the coral reefs. Before cleaned by collectors, the shell is covered with a fuzzy outer layer of hairy periostracum.

Plate 57. The so-called Maple Leaf is an extraordinary Japanese shell characterized by its flattened maple-leaflike outline. Known as *Biplex perca* Perry, this strange three-inch shell has found its way into the world of design and jewelry because of its unique sculpture and architecture.

Murex, Doves, and Drupe Shells

Plates 58 and 59. The Rose-branched Murex of the Indian Ocean is probably the most beautiful of the huge family of spiny *Murex* rock shells. This five-inch spectacular creation is characterized by exploding fronds that are tipped with delicate shades of lavender. *Murex palma-rosae* Lamarck, long a collector's item, comes from the area of Ceylon. In ancient times other species of *Murex* produced a purple dye that was used to color wool and cotton of the Phoenicians and Egyptians. Royal Tyrian Purple dye came from the animals of these shells, and during Roman times the dye was so expensive and exclusive that the Emperor Nero forbade its use by common people.

Plate 60. Vying in beauty with the *Murex* shells are their near relatives, the *Latiaxis* shells. Here is shown Dunker's Latiaxis, *Latiaxis dunkeri* Kuroda and Habe, a two-inch-long species from Japan. There is so much variation in these shells that there has been an overabundance of scientific names applied to the numerous ecological forms. Another species is shown in Plate 66.

Plate 61. The common rock-dwelling Beggar Engina, *Engina mendicaria* Linné, of the Indo-Pacific, is readily recognized by the black-and-yellow striped motif. It is only a third of an inch in size.

Plate 62. More delicate and with finer spiral bands is the less common *Engina lineata* Lamarck of the Indo-Pacific, also less than a third of an inch.

Plate 63. *Phos senticosus* (Linné) is a commonly dredged buccinid snail of the Indo-Pacific, usually only one inch in length.

Plate 64. The family of mud snails, Nassariidae, is abundant throughout the tropical world, usually in intertidal, muddy areas. This half-inch-long species, *Nassarius suturalis* (Lamarck), is common in Australia.

Plate 65. Dove shells are extraordinarily beautiful, although most of the species are quite small. Here, the Dancing Dove Shell, *Anachis terpsichore* (Sowerby), is a denizen of Indian shores.

Plate 66. Among the numerous forms of Latiaxis Shells is this unusual form of *Latiaxis latipinnatus* Azuma, a two-inch jewel from deep water off southern Japan.

Plate 67. Frilled and spined, the gorgeous Yellow Drupe of the western Pacific Ocean, *Drupa grossularia* Röding, is a common inhabitant of tropical rocky shores. It is an inch in size.

Plate 68. The Lightning Dove Shell, *Pyrene fulgurans* (Lamarck), is a quarter-inch variable species from the Indo-Pacific.

Plate 69. *Pyrene tringa* (Lamarck) from Japan, a tiny Dove Shell of shallow waters, sports a strong zigzag pattern.

Plate 70. The Common Pacific Drupe, *Drupa ricinus* (Linné), is abundant on wave-dashed coral shores of the entire Indo-Pacific region. It seldom exceeds an inch in size.

Plate 71 and 72. The Jewel Mud Snail, *Nassarius gemmulatus* (Lamarck), is an inch-long study in beautiful, bulbous beading. This is a common Indian Ocean species.

Miters and Olives

Plates 73 and 74. The fabulous little Tiara Miter, *Cancilla filaris* (Linné), has three or four strong spiral rows of dark beads surrounding its whorls. This inch-long gem is common in the Indo-Pacific.

Plate 75. The contrast of the raised white ridges and the orange background of this small miter of the tropical Pacific characterizes *Mitra pediculus* Lamarck, the three-quarter-inch Flea Miter.

Plate 76. King of the miter shells is this common but stunning *Mitra mitra* Linné, a three- to five-inch shell known to Europe since the earliest days of exploration. It is popularly known as the Episcopal Miter.

Plate 77. Rare and choice is this *Swainsonia variegata* (Gmelin), an inch-and-a-half-long miter, noted for the deep but minute punctures in the surface of the shell. It lives in sandy bays in the Indo-Pacific region.

Plate 78. The Three-colored Olive, *Oliva tricolor* Lamarck, is a common species in the southwest Pacific. It reaches a length of two inches.

Plates 79 and 80. The Bulbous Olive of the western section of the Indian Ocean is characterized by a spiral swelling on the base of the columella. The color patterns are very variable. Here is shown an unusual zebra-striped form from the Gulf of Aden. His scientific name is *Oliva bulbosa* (Röding).

The Molluscan Aristocrats

No groups of seashells have been more avidly sought after by collectors than the cones, volutes, and harps. Some of the highest prices, a few over the $2000 mark, have been paid for rare cones. The majority of the four hundred-or-so known species of *Conus* came from the shallow tropical waters of the Indian and southwest Pacific oceans. Not all cone specimens are as bright and colorful in nature as shown here, for many of them have a natural chitinous outer covering, the periostracum. This protects the shell from abrasion and from being readily found by fish. It may be removed by soaking the shell in a strong bleach for a few hours.

All of the cones are armed with a microscopic hypodermic needle inside the proboscis. Behind the tooth is a long duct containing a very strong venom. The cone snail is capable of stinging a small fish or marine worm, paralyzing it, and then drawing its victim into its esophagus. Although this harpoon apparatus is mainly for obtaining food, a cone will use it for defensive purposes, particularly against the octopus and other carnivorous mollusks. There have been ten authentic cases of human death resulting from cone stings. All fatal cases have been in the tropical Indo-Pacific area. The most dangerous is the Geography Cone, which must be picked up with care.

The glossy, beautifully ribbed harp shells are common inhabitants of South Pacific sand bottoms. The foot of the harp is enormous and as colorful as the shell itself.

Plate 81. The Marble Cone of the Indo-Pacific area is moderately common in gravel and sand in the shallow waters near coral reefs. They reach a length of about three inches. In nature, the outside of the shell of *Conus marmoreus* Linné has a tan, chitinous covering.

Plate 82. The Admiral Cone, *Conus ammiralis* Linné, is a handsome collector's item from the southwest Pacific. In the 1700s collectors paid high prices for this exquisite and uncommon species that reaches a length of two inches. The Admiral Cone walks about at night over coral gravel bottoms. Its outer covering is very thin and varnishlike.

Plates 83 and 84. Of the dozen species of Harpidae, the two-inch-long Minor Harp of the Indo-Pacific, *Harpa amouretta* Röding, is the commonest. It feeds on crustaceans.

Plates 85 and 86. The Striate Cone, *Conus striatus* Linné, has a history of having stung humans, although its venom is not very powerful. This three-inch species is moderately common throughout the Indian and tropical western Pacific Oceans.

Plate 87. The Flea Cone, *Conus pulicarius* Hwass, is one of the commonest sand-dwelling members of its family. It is found throughout the Indo-Pacific and usually grows to about one and a half inches in size.

Plate 88. The vast array of genera and species in the turrid family makes this group too bewildering for the average collector. However, the deep-water Star Turrids are considered collector's items. This is the Beautiful Star Turrid, *Cochlespira pulchella* (Schepman), an inch-long variable shell from the western Pacific.

Plate 89. There are more than two hundred species of volutes. Australia possesses more species than any other country. The Beautiful Volute, *Cymbiolacca pulchra* (Sowerby), is three inches long and one of the most attractive of the shallow-water Queensland species.

Plate 90. Scarcely resembling a conventional molluscan shell, this tiny glassy shell belongs to the pelagic group of univalves known as pteropods. Floating through the open seas by the millions, this species, *Cavolina trispinosa* Lesueur, keeps itself afloat and swimming by fleshy, flaplike wings. It is the main food of many oceanic fish and whales.

Plate 91. Most famous of all the turrids is nature's gift to the architect, the Miraculous Thatcheria from Japan, *Thatcheria mirabilis* Angas. This three-inch deep-water shell comes from off the coast of central Japan. It is lightweight but strong. Formerly considered a great rarity, it is now brought up in fishermen's nets in moderate numbers.

Other Classes of Mollusks

It is unfortunate that the popular univalve snails attract the most attention from conchologists, for the other groups of mollusks are equally beautiful and perhaps even more interesting from a biological standpoint. There are six or seven other classes of mollusks, but the most important ones are illustrated here. The *bivalves* include the clams, oysters, and scallops, of which there are perhaps 15,000 species to be found in the ocean and in large bodies of fresh water. The *chitons* or Amphineura include specialized snail-like creatures having eight shelly plates, held together by a surrounding girdle. They are confined to marine waters and live on rocks. The *cephalopods* are the most advanced of the mollusks. Squids, octopuses and nautiluses have enlarged brains, efficient eyes, and suckered tentacles. The *scaphopods* or tusk shells are simple mollusks, having a tubular shell open at both ends resembling miniature elephant tusks. The tusks are marine and live buried in sand with one end protruding above the surface. There are only about four hundred known species.

Plate 92. The two valves of clams are locked together by intricate teeth built into the hinge side of the clam shell. Some bivalves have very simple hinges, but the taxodont clams, such as this Divaricate Nut Clam, *Acila divaricata* (Hinds), has a splendid row of comblike teeth. This is an inch-long cold-water species from the north Pacific.

Plate 93. Scallops have been used by man for many hundreds of generations, not only as food, but also as a religious and sex symbol. Aphrodite, the Greek goddess of love, and the Roman equivalent, Venus, were born from a scallop shell. The scallop became associated with

Christ's apostle Saint James, whose bones were presumably buried at Compostela, Spain. For centuries pilgrims visiting his grave were given a scallop shell to symbolize the completion of their religious trip. Similarly, knights who engaged in the Crusades to the Near East to fight the Saracens used a scallop shell to signify that they had participated in their holy war. Many of the family crests of today's English nobility have scallop shells to indicate that their ancestors went in search of the Holy Grail. Today the scallop is used as a symbol for one of the leading oil companies. The inch-long Spectacular Scallop shown here is *Chlamys spectabilis* (Reeve), a daintily sculptured bivalve from the Indo-Pacific.

Plate 94. This two-inch chiton resembles a pill bug, but it is a snail-like mollusk that clings to seashore rocks. The eight shelly plates are held together by the muscular girdle which in the case of this southern Australian species is covered with tiny shelly beads. *Ischnochiton lineolatus* Blainville is a plentiful species.

Plate 95. The shelly plates of chitons have very characteristic sculpturing. *Rhyssoplax calliozonus* Pilsbry, a two-inch chiton, lives on smooth rocks in clean oceanic pools along the shore of southern Australia.

Plate 96. The intricate detail of the sculpturing of a chiton is used to distinguish species. This is an intimate view of *Rhyssoplax jugosus* (Gould), which lives under stones in the intertidal areas of southeast Australia.

Plates 97 and 98. Scallop shells are rather brittle, and they are strengthened by ribs which, in turn, have an intricate complex of scales and reinforcing threads. The Mantle Scallop, *Chlamys pallium* (Linné), is a common Indo-Pacific species reaching a diameter of about two inches.

Plate 99. Although there are about four hundred species of tusk shells in the world, they do not show much variation in their basic shape. Here is one of the most elegant of the tusks, *Dentalium crocinum* Dall, from Japan. This graceful sliver is more than three and a half inches in length. It was dredged from a sandy bottom about a hundred fathoms below the surface of the ocean.

Plate 100. The Chambered Nautilus inspired the poet Oliver Wendell Holmes to compose a majestic poem. To the left is the rare *Nautilus macromphalus* Sowerby, known only from the area around New Caledonia. The shell to the right is *Nautilus pompilius* Linné, the common Pearly Nautilus of the southwest Pacific. It has been cut in half to show the internal chambers that keep this creature buoyed up. Below is a Paper Nautilus, *Argonauta argo* Linné, which is not at all related to the Nautiluses, but is, in fact, the egg case of an octopuslike animal that lives a pelagic life on the high seas.

Plate 101. The Venus Comb Murex, resembling the cleaned bones of a fish, is a challenge to man's understanding of the manufacture of spiny shell material. Each of the long, slender spines is tubular. The mantle edge of the snail grows into small pointed protuberances. Around these the bases of the spines are built. Soon the protuberances grow into lengthened filaments with shell material being exuded and hardened around them as they extend out farther and farther. When the spines are at their final length, the fleshy tubes within the spine are gradually reabsorbed, cell by cell, into the main part of the mantle.

Although these long spines may serve as a protection against marauding fish or other shell-drilling snails, and possibly as a coat hanger for camouflaging seaweeds, they are a nuisance to the murex snail itself. Crawling about over rough sea bottom is especially difficult, but in order to lift its long spines over obstacles, the murex rises high on its long, pedestal-shaped foot and then glides forward. An additional problem involves the natural coiling growth of the shell. To enlarge, the shell is built up in the region of the aperture of the shell. New whorls are added. But the siphon cannot be added to, except at the tip end. Therefore, the fleshy tube has to be withdrawn, the old siphonal canal abandoned, and when the shell has moved its outer lip forward, the tube is once more extended in order to manufacture a new siphonal canal.

As the snail builds new whorls, it faces the problem of formerly built rows of spines. Unless they are removed in some fashion, further whorl expansion is impossible. This is done by two methods, the first being the dissolving action of the part of the mantle lying next to the inner lip. The second method is by the snail using its strong radular teeth to rasp off the spines.

The Venus Comb Murex, *Murex pecten* Lightfoot, lives in warm tropical waters on a bottom of rubble and pebbles, usually at a depth of thirty to one hundred feet. Its geographical occurrence is from the east coast of Africa to Japan and Melanesia, although it reaches its zenith of size (four to five inches) and perfection in the central Philippines.

Figure 8. Chemical odors given off by starfish elicit violent reactions from most mollusks. Once touched by the tubular feet of the carnivorous, mollusk-eating star-fish, a *Nassarius* mud snail makes frantic lashings with its foot in order to escape from its enemy.

Bibliography

This is a brief list of some of the readily available, popular books on conchology. Many of these references contain more extensive bibliographies on the subject which, today, is encompassed by many hundreds of volumes.

General Reading

Abbott, R. Tucker. *Kingdom of the Seashell.* New York: Crown, 1972.

Dance, S. Peter. *Shell Collecting—an Illustrated History.* Berkeley, Calif.: University of California Press, 1966.

Johnstone, Kathleen Y. *Sea Treasure.* Boston: Houghton Mifflin Co., 1957.

Stix, Hugh and Marguerite, and R. T. Abbott. *The Shell—Five Hundred Million Years of Inspired Design.* New York: Harry N. Abrams, Inc., 1968.

Travers, L. A. *The Romance of Shells in Nature and Art.* New York: M. Barrows, 1962.

Field Guides to Identification

Abbott, R. Tucker. *Sea Shells of the World.* New York: Golden Press, 1962.

Abbott, R. Tucker. *American Seashells.* New York: Van Nostrand-Reinhold, 1955.

Abbott, R. Tucker. *Seashells of North America.* New York: Golden Press, 1968.

Burgess, C. W. *The Living Cowries.* South Brunswick, N.J.: A. S. Barnes and Co., 1970.

Habe, Tadashige. *Shells of Japan.* Color Books no. 24. Osaka, Japan: Hoikusha Co., 1971.

Keen, A. Myra. *Marine Shells of Tropical West America.* Stanford, Calif.: Stanford University Press, 1971.

Powell, A. W. B. *Shells of New Zealand.* Auckland: Whitcombe and Tombs, Ltd., 1957.

Warmke, G. L., and R. T. Abbott. *Caribbean Seashells.* Wynnewood, Pa.: Livingston Co., 1961.

Weaver, C. S., and John E. du Pont. *The Living Volutes.* Greenville, Dela.: Delaware Museum of Natural History, 1970.

Wilson, B. R. and K. Gillett. *Australian Shells.* Sydney: A. H. and A. W. Reed, 1971.

INDEX

Figures in italics refer to the plates.